The Great Texas Cookbook

Rustling Up Food Cowboy-Style

Table of Contents

Introduction 4

Appetizers 6

    Tex-Mex Shrimp Cocktail 7

    Cowboy Caviar 9

    Queso Dip 11

    Jalapeno Poppers 14

    Salsa with Heat 17

Main Meals 19

    Slow Cooker Pork Ribs 20

    Slow Cooker Pulled Pork 23

    Sloppy Joes 26

    Salpicon 28

    Slow Cooker Smoked Beef Brisket 30

    Chicken Fried Steak with Gravy 32

    Taco Salad 35

    Texas Patty Melts 38

    Grilled Tex-Mex Burgers 41

    Tex-Mex Enchiladas 44

    Bunkhouse Stew 47

    BBQ Chicken 49

    Smothered Chicken 51

    Chicken Quesadillas 54

Soups and Stews *57*

    Texas Turkey Soup 58

    Texas Chili 61

    Corn Chowder 63

    Texas-Style Gumbo 66

Seafood *69*

    Fried Catfish 70

    Spicy Shrimp Po' Boy 73

    Veracruz Shrimp 76

Sides *79*

    Coleslaw 80

    Tex-Mex Corn 82

    Jalapeno Yams 84

    Ranch Potato Salad 87

    Pinto Beans 89

Dessert *91*

    Oatmeal Cookies 92

    Texas Sheet Cake 95

Introduction

Texas is both a place and a state of mind. Everything is big in Texas, including its meals. In Texas, food is all about the joy of eating. This Great State of Texas Cookbook brings that joy into your kitchen.

Texas' history and connection with Mexico still influences most of its dishes. Hot seasoning, jalapeno peppers, tortillas, tomatoes, beans, and corn find their way into most meals.

And since Texas is cattle country, a lot of those meals involve beef. It's a great combination.

Barbeques are not only a Texas tradition, but barbequing meat originated in Texas. It started with the South American tradition of burying beef and other meats in the ground with hot coals. When Germans and Czechs immigrated to Texas in the 1800s, they smoked their leftover, tough pieces of beef to keep it fresh

These leftovers became a staple for cowboys and migrant workers. It was considered "poor man's" food. Poor migrants discovered that simmering these low-grade meats in a sauce made them quite tender. Add a few Texas staples, and the bar-b-que was born.

The "poor man's food" is now beloved by everyone. But it's hard to think of BBQ and not think of Texas. This Great State of Texas Cookbook has appetizers straight from the border and main meals with a kick. Even side dishes are prepared with spices to give them a special taste. Treat your family to some Texas-style love. Remember that the spices can be adjusted to individual tastes.

Appetizers

Tex-Mex Shrimp Cocktail

Not your usual shrimp cocktail. This one packs a Texas-style punch.

Cooking Time: 0

Servings: 8

Ingredients:

- 1 lb. cooked shrimp
- 3 chopped celery stalks
- 1 small cubed tomato

- ¼ cup chopped scallions
- ¼ cup cubed avocado
- 2 chopped serrano peppers
- 1 cup prepared salsa
- 1 tbsp. white vinegar
- 1 tbsp. lime juice

Directions:

1. Combine the shrimp, celery, tomato, scallions, avocado, serrano peppers, and salsa in a bowl.

2. Combine the vinegar and lime juice and drizzle over the shrimp cocktail.

Cowboy Caviar

The flavors really meld if you let this salad sit for about half an hour before serving.

Cooking Time: 0

Servings: 8

Ingredients:

- 25 oz. drained and rinsed black beans
- 4 diced tomatoes
- 2 cups of thawed frozen corn kernels
- ¼ cup chopped sweet onion
- 2 deseeded and chopped jalapeno peppers
- Salt and pepper to taste
- ¼ cup olive oil
- 3 tbsp. lime juice
- 1 tbsp. sugar
- 1 tsp. chili powder
- 1 tsp. cumin
- 2/3 cup of chopped cilantro

Directions:

1. Mix the beans, tomatoes, corn, onion and jalapeno peppers in a big bowl.

2. Season with salt and pepper.

3. Combine the remaining ingredients and drizzle over the beans.

4. Refrigerate for 30 minutes.

Queso Dip

Serve this great cheesy dip with some tortilla chips.

Cooking Time: 16 minutes

Servings: 12

Ingredients:

- 2 halved and seeded poblano peppers
- 2 halved and seeded Anaheim peppers

- ½ cup diced fire-roasted chilies
- 2 cups shredded white cheddar cheese
- 3 diced plum tomatoes
- 1 diced onion
- 1 tsp. cumin
- ½ cup half and half

Directions

1. Preheat the broiler.

2. Place the poblano and Anaheim pepper on a lined baking sheet.

3. Cook the peppers for 8 minutes, until they are blackened.

4. Place the peppers in a plastic bag for 20 minutes.

5. Remove the skin from the peppers and dice.

6. Combined the chopped peppers, chili peppers, shredded cheese, tomatoes, onion, and cumin in a pan.

7. Stir in the half and half and combine well.

8. Add more liquid if necessary.

9. Simmer on low for 8 minutes. The cheese should be melted.

Jalapeno Poppers

These are a hit at any party.

Cooking Time: 20 minutes

Servings: 60

Ingredients:

- 1 lb. ground pork
- 1 chopped small onion
- 8 oz. cream cheese
- 1 cup shredded cheddar cheese
- ¼ tsp. cumin
- ¼ tsp. chili powder
- 30 jalapeno peppers
- 30 bacon slices
- 1 tbsp. honey

Directions:

1. Preheat the oven to 375 degrees.

2. Add the ground pork to a skillet and brown for 5 minutes.

3. Drain the pork of fat and place in a bowl.

4. Stir in the cream cheese, cheddar cheese, cumin and chili powder

5. Slice the jalapenos lengthwise and deseed.

6. Fill each jalapeno half with the filling.

7. Either microwave or fry the bacon slices for a few minutes to rid them of some of the fat.

8. Brush each bacon slice with a bit of honey.

9. Cut the bacon slices in half and wrap each half around a jalapeno half.

10. Secure the jalapeno popper with some toothpicks.

11. Place the jalapenos on a baking dish.

12. Bake for 20 minutes.

Salsa with Heat

Can't party in Texas without some good salsa. Serve this with chips. This is fairly hot, so adjust the heat to your own taste. If you use canned tomatoes, please drain them thoroughly to prevent the salsa from becoming too soggy.

Cooking Time: 8

Servings: 18

Ingredients:

- 1 lb. diced Roma tomatoes
- 1 diced onion

- 3 minced garlic cloves
- 2 chopped jalapeno pepper
- 1 tsp. lemon juice or to taste
- 1 tsp. cider vinegar
- Salt to taste
- 2 sliced red chili pepper
- ¼ cup cilantro

Directions:

Toss the ingredients in a blender and process to your desired consistency.

Main Meals

Slow Cooker Pork Ribs

These are fall-off-the-bone tender and so easy to prepare in the slow cooker. It's the spice rub that really brings out the flavor.

Ingredients:

Cooking Time: 8 hours 5 minutes

Servings: 10

Ingredients:

- 6 lb. country-style spareribs
- 1 cup white sugar
- 2 tbsp. salt
- 1 tbsp. pepper
- 1 tbsp. smoky paprika
- 1 tbsp. garlic powder
- 2 tbsp. olive oil
- 1 chopped onion
- 3 minced garlic cloves
- 4 cups BBQ sauce
- 1 tsp. liquid smoke

Directions:

1. Combine the sugar and spices in a bowl.

2. Rub the mix all over the ribs.

3. Place the ribs on a cooking sheet and refrigerate overnight.

4. Heat the oil in a skillet and sauté the onion and garlic for 5 minutes.

5. Place the ribs in the slow cooker and top with the onion and garlic.

6. Stir in the BBQ sauce and liquid smoke.

7. Cook on low for 8 hours.

Slow Cooker Pulled Pork

Served these on a roll for a delicious sandwich.

Cooking Time: 11 hours

Servings: 8

Ingredients:

- 4-lb. pork roast
- 2 cup barbeque sauce (you can mix sweet and hickory-smoked)
- ¼ apple cider vinegar

- ¼ cup chicken broth
- 2 tsp. soy sauce
- ¼ cup brown sugar
- 1 tbsp. mustard
- 1 tsp. garlic powder
- 1 tsp. onion powder
- 1 chopped onion
- 3 minced garlic cloves
- 8 rolls
- 3 tbsp. butter

Directions:

1. Place the roast into a slow cooker.

2. Combine the BBQ sauce, vinegar, broth and soy sauce and pour over the roast

3. Combine the sugar, mustard, garlic powder, onion powder, onion and garlic and stir into the liquid.

4. Cook on low for 10 hours.

5. Remove the pork roast and use a fork to shred the meat.

6. Place the shredded meat back into the slow cooker and cook for 1 more hour.

7. Butter the rolls (you can toast them first) and fill the rolls with the shredded pork.

Sloppy Joes

Old-fashioned and sloppy. Just the way everyone loves them.

Cooking Time: 25 minutes

Servings: 6

Ingredients:

- 1 tbsp. olive oil
- 2 lb. ground beef
- 1 chopped onion
- 1 chopped bell pepper

- Salt and pepper to taste
- 2 cups tomato sauce
- ¼ cup ketchup
- ¼ cup apple cider vinegar
- 2 tbsp. steak sauce
- ¼ cup brown sugar
- 2 tbsp. BBQ sauce
- 6 hamburger buns

Directions:

1. Heat the olive oil in a large skillet

2. Brown the beef for 5 minutes.

3. Stir in the onion and bell pepper and season with salt and pepper.

4. Cook on low for 5 minutes.

5. Stir in the remaining ingredients except for the buns.

6. Simmer for 15 minutes.

7. Toast the hamburger buns and top with helpings of sloppy joe.

Salpicon

Shredded beef salad El Paso-style. Serve with some corn tortillas.

Cooking Time: 5 hours

Servings: 12

Ingredients:

- 5-lb. beef roast
- Salt and pepper to taste

- 4 cups beef broth
- 1 chopped onion
- 3 chopped chipotle peppers
- ¾ cup olive oil
- ¼ cup white vinegar
- 3 minced garlic cloves
- 1 cup Rotel tomatoes

Directions:

1. Season the roast with salt and pepper.

2. Place the roast and onions with a Dutch oven.

3. Pour the broth over the roast.

4. Cook on low for 5 hours, until the roast is done.

5. Add more broth if necessary

6. Remove the roast and shred with a fork. Retain 2 cups of liquid.

7. Combine the onion, chipotle peppers, olive oil, vinegar, garlic and Rotel tomatoes in a blender and process.

8. Stir in the reserved liquid and toss with the shredded meat.

Slow Cooker Smoked Beef Brisket

This has a nice smoky taste. Serve with mashed potatoes or use for sandwiches.

Cooking Time: 8 hours

Servings: 4

Ingredients:

- 1 tbsp. smoked paprika
- 1 tbsp. pepper
- 1 tbsp. salt
- 2 tbsp. brown sugar
- 1 tsp. chili powder
- 2 lb. beef brisket

- 1 cup barbeque sauce
- ¾ cup beer
- 1 tsp. Worcestershire sauce
- Dash of liquid smoke
- 1 tbsp. cider vinegar
- 2 sliced onions

Directions:

1. Combine the spices, salt, pepper and brown sugar in a bowl

2. Rub the spice mix over the beef brisket.

3. Refrigerate the brisket for 12 hours

4. Combine the barbeque sauce, beer, Worcestershire sauce, liquid smoke and cider vinegar in a bowl.

5. Pour the liquid into the slow cooker

6. Place the brisket in the slow cooker and top with onions.

7. Cook on low for 8 hours.

8. Shred the brisket and serve with the sauce.

Chicken Fried Steak with Gravy

A southwest staple. The gravy is perfect with mashed potatoes.

Cooking Time: 12 minutes

Servings: 4

Ingredients:

- 4 small cube steaks
- Salt and pepper to taste
- ½ cup white flour
- ¼ tsp. garlic powder
- ¼ tsp. paprika
- 2 beaten eggs
- 3 tbsp. vegetable oil
- 1 cup milk
- ½ cup white flour

Directions:

1. Salt and pepper the cube steaks.

2. Combine the flour, garlic powder and paprika in a bowl.

3. Place the beaten eggs in a second bowl.

4. Dredge the steaks through the flour, then the eggs. Dredge through the flour a second time.

5. Heat the oil in a skillet.

6. Fry the steaks 4 minutes on each side.

7. If there isn't enough oil left, add some to the skillet.

8. Scrape the brown bits from the bottom of the skillet.

9. Drain the steaks on a paper towel.

10. Stir the flour into the oil

11. Add the milk, keep stirring, and season with lots of pepper.

12. Cook for 4 minutes or until gravy is smooth.

13. Pour the gravy over the steaks.

Taco Salad

Who doesn't want a taco salad when the weather is hot?

Cooking Time: 5 minutes

Servings: 6

Ingredients:

- 1 lb. ground beef
- 1 diced onion
- 1 tsp. taco seasoning mix

- Salt and pepper to taste
- Head of chopped lettuce
- 2 cups shredded Cheddar cheese
- 1 cup drained canned kidney beans
- ¼ cup chopped black olives
- 1 cubed avocado
- 1 cup mild salsa
- 5 tbsp. Ranch dressing
- 3 tbsp. sour cream
- 1 cup crunched ranch-flavored tortilla chips

Directions

1. Add the beef and onion to a skillet and mix in the taco seasoning.

2. Brown for 5 minutes or until the beef is no longer pink.

3. Set aside and season with salt and pepper.

4. Rip the lettuce to pieces and place into a salad bowl.

5. Add the cheese, beans, olives, avocado and salsa. Toss the salad well.

6. Combine the Ranch dressing with the sour cream and stir into the salad to coat.

7. Top with the tortilla chips.

Texas Patty Melts

These are great, and they're the best when you use Texas Toast bread.

Cooking Time:

Servings:

Ingredients:

- 1 lb. ground beef
- Salt and pepper to taste
- 1 sliced and grilled onion
- 1 chopped chipotle pepper

- 2 tbsp. sour cream
- 2 tbsp. mayonnaise
- 1 diced chipotle pepper in adobo sauce
- 8 sliced of Texas Toast bread
- 4 slices pepper jack cheese
- 4 sliced cheddar cheese
- 2 tbsp. butter

Directions:

1. Combine the ground beef, salt and pepper and 1 diced chipotle pepper,

2. Add the beef to a skillet and cook until the meat is just a bit pink.

3. Create 4 separate patties.

4. Mix together the chili seasoning mix, 1 diced chipotle peppers and ground beef with adobo sauce in a bowl. Divide the mixture evenly into 4 patties.

5. Stir together the mayonnaise, sour cream.

6. Spread the dressing on 4 of the bread slices

7. Add 1 slice of pepper jack cheese and 1 slice of cheddar cheese to the 4 bread slices.

8. Heat the butter in a skillet

9. Add 1 beef patty on top of the cheese slices.

10. Cover the 4 slices with the remaining 4 slices of Texas Toast bread

11. Fry/grill the sandwiches for 5 minutes each side.

Grilled Tex-Mex Burgers

You'll never go to McDonald's again.

Cooking Time: 10 minutes

Servings: 4

Ingredients:

- ½ cup mayonnaise
- ¼ tsp. Cajun seasoning
- ¼ tsp. garlic powder.
- ¼ tsp. garlic salt
- 1 ½ lb. ground beef

- 2 chopped and seeded jalapeno peppers
- 1 diced onion
- 2 minced garlic cloves
- 1 tsp. Cajun seasoning
- 1 tsp. soy sauce
- Dash of red pepper flakes
- 4 slices Monterey Jack cheese
- 4 hamburger buns
- 2 sliced tomatoes
- Bunch of lettuce

Directions:

1. Preheat a grill for medium-high heat.

2. Combine the mayonnaise, Cajun seasoning, garlic powder and garlic salt in a bowl.

3. In a larger bowl, combine the remaining ingredients except the buns, sliced tomatoes and lettuce. Use your hands to really mix well.

4. Create 4 patties.

5. Oil the surface of the grill and add the beef patties.

6. Grill for 5 minutes on each side.

7. Grill the buns for 2 minutes just to toast them.

8. Spread the spicy mayonnaise on each side of the buns.

9. Add a hamburger patty to each bun and top with tomato slices and some lettuce.

Tex-Mex Enchiladas

Enchiladas are frequently pretty mild. But not if you're from Texas!

Cooking Time: 50 minutes

Servings: 6

Ingredients:

- 2 lbs. ground beef
- 1 diced onion
- 3 minced garlic cloves
- 2 tbsp. chili powder
- 2 tbsp. paprika

- 2 tbsp. cumin
- 1 tsp. coriander
- Salt to taste
- 1 cup tomato sauce
- 2 chopped green chilis
- 4 cups chicken stock
- 12 corn tortillas
- 4 cups shredded Colby Jack cheese

Directions:

1. Preheat the oven to 350 degrees.

2. Sauté the onion and garlic for 5 minutes.

3. Stir the ground beef into the mixture and brown the beef for 5 minutes.

4. Drain the grease.

5. Add all of the seasoning, tomato sauce and broth and combine well.

6. Simmer for 15 minutes.

7. Heat the tortillas in the oven for 5 minutes while the sauce simmers.

8. Divide the beef filling between the tortilla and roll them up.

9. Transfer the tortillas to a 9 x 13 baking dish and top with the sauce.

10. Sprinkle with the shredded cheese.

11. Bake for 25 minutes.

Bunkhouse Stew

This is the kind of use-what-you-have type of stew that works great on the ranch. Think of your slow cooker as a campfire.

Cooking Time: 8 hours 8 minutes

Servings: 12

Ingredients:

- 2 lbs. stew meat
- 1 cup sliced andouille sausage
- 4 minced garlic cloves

- 1 chopped onion
- 28 oz. drained diced tomatoes
- 1 cup tomato sauce
- 1 diced chili pepper
- 2 diced jalapeno peppers
- 4 cups beef broth
- 1 tsp. cumin
- 1 tsp. chili powder
- Dash of cayenne pepper
- Salt and pepper to taste
- 3 peeled and diced potatoes
- 30 oz. canned kidney beans

Directions:

1. Add the beef, sausage, onion and garlic to a skillet and sauté for 8 minutes.

2. Drain off the grease.

3. Place these ingredients in a slow cooker and stir in everything else except the potatoes and beans.

4. Cook on low for 5 hours.

5. Add the potatoes and beans and cook for 3 more hours.

BBQ Chicken

This couldn't be easier to prepare. You can serve this over rice or make fantastic sandwiches.

Cooking Time: 45 minutes

Servings: 8

Ingredients:

- 8 boneless, skinless chicken breasts
- 2 cup BBQ sauce

Directions:

1. Preheat the oven to 350 degrees.

2. Arrange the chicken on a baking dish.

3. Pour the BBQ sauce over the chicken

4. Bake for 30 minutes.

5. Transfer the chicken to a platter and shred.

6. Return the chicken to the sauce, stir, and cook an additional 15 minutes.

Smothered Chicken

The cayenne pepper adds a bit of Texas heat. If you wish, you can also add a diced bell pepper.

Cooking Time: 40 minutes

Servings: 8

Ingredients:

- ½ cup butter
- 2 lb. bone-in skin-on chicken thighs
- Salt and pepper to taste
- ¼ tsp. poultry seasoning
- ½ cup white flour
- 2 chopped onions
- 2 cups sliced mushrooms
- 3 minced garlic cloves
- ¼ cup flour
- 3 cups chicken broth
- Dash of cayenne pepper
- ¼ tsp. garlic salt
- ¼ tsp. garlic powder
- 1 tbsp. Gravy Master
- Salt and pepper to taste

Directions:

1. Season the chicken with salt, pepper and poultry seasoning.

2. Dredge the chicken through the flour.

3. Melt the butter in a skillet and brown the chicken for 5 minutes each side. Set aside.

4. Retain 2 tbsp. of butter in the skillet.

5. Sauté the onion, mushrooms and garlic for 5 minutes

6. Add the flour and stir well.

7. Pour the broth into the skillet and stir in the cayenne pepper, garlic salt, garlic powder, Gravy Master, salt and pepper.

8. Bring the broth to a boil.

9. Transfer the chicken back to the skillet and simmer for 30 minutes.

10. Serve with mashed potatoes.

Chicken Quesadillas

These are wonderful spicy quesadillas. We bake them, but if you prefer, you can also fry them when they are assembled. Caramelizing the onions for a long time is critical to bringing out their sweet flavor.

Cooking Time: 1 hour

Servings: 8

Ingredients:

- 3 tbsp. olive oil
- 1 sliced onion
- 1 chopped and seeded jalapeno pepper
- 2 cups shredded cooked chicken (if using left-over BBQ chicken, omit the BBQ sauce)
- ½ cup BBQ sauce
- 1 tsp. chili powder
- 2 cups shredded mixed cheese
- 8 flour tortillas

Directions:

1. Preheat the oven to 350 degrees.

2. Heat 2 tbsp. oil in a skillet and caramelize the onions on low heat for 40 minutes. Set aside.

3. Add the remaining oil to the skillet and stir in the shredded chicken, BBQ sauce, and chili powder.

4. Cook for 5 minutes.

5. Fill each tortilla with the chicken, caramelized onion, and cheese.

6. Fold one side of the tortilla over the other side.

7. Place the tortilla on a baking sheet and bake for 15 minutes.

8. Place the tortillas on a plate and cut in half.

Soups and Stews

Texas Turkey Soup

You can make this delicious soup from leftover Thanksgiving turkey, but smoked turkey legs add a nice dimension to this soup.

Cooking Time: 47 minutes

Servings: 6

Ingredients:

- 1 tbsp. olive oil
- 1 diced onion
- 4 diced garlic cloves

- 1 tsp. chili powder
- ½ tsp. cumin
- ½ tsp. thyme
- 5 cups chicken broth
- 14 oz. can diced tomatoes
- 1 cup Rotel tomatoes
- 4 cups shredded cooked turkey
- 2 cup drained canned black beans
- 1 cup frozen corn
- 1/3 cup sour cream
- 1 chopped jalapeno pepper – optional

Toppings:

- Tortilla chips
- Chopped scallions
- Shredded cheese
- Sour cream

Directions:

1. Heat the olive oil in a soup pot and sauté the onion for 5 minutes.

2. Stir in the garlic, chili powder, cumin and thyme and cook for 2 minutes.

3. Add the broth, diced tomatoes. Rotel tomatoes, and turkey.

4. Stir thoroughly and add the beans, corn, sour cream and jalapeno pepper.

5. Bring to a boil and simmer for 40 minutes.

6. Serve the soup with the toppings.

Texas Chili

Texas is beef country. True Texas-style chili contains no beans.

Cooking Time: 1 hour 35 minutes

Servings: 8

Ingredients:

- 3 lb. cubed beef
- 2 tbsp. flour
- 2 tbsp. olive oil
- 1 chopped onion

- 4 minced garlic cloves
- 4 tbsp. chili powder
- 1 tsp. cumin
- 1 tbsp. oregano
- 2 cans beef broth
- Salt and pepper to taste
- 1 cup beer
- 1 tbsp. lime juice

Directions:

1. Heat the oil in a large skillet.

2. Place the beef and flour in a plastic bag and shake to coat.

3. Transfer the beef to the skillet and brown on all side for 5 minutes.

4. Stir in the onion, garlic, chili powder, cumin and oregano.

5. Make sure the beef is coated with the spices.

6. Pour in the broth, beer and lime juice.

7. Season with salt and pepper and bring the broth to a boil.

8. Cover partially and simmer for 1 hour and 30minutes.

Corn Chowder

This is not your wimpy East Coast corn chowder.

Cooking Time: 15 minutes

Servings: 6

- 2 tbsp. olive oil
- 1 large chopped onion
- 3 minced garlic cloves
- 2 tbsp. white flour
- 1 tsp. chili powder
- 1 tsp. coriander
- ½ tsp. cayenne pepper

- Salt and pepper to taste
- 2 cups mild picante sauce
- 3 cups chicken broth
- 1 large peeled and cubed potato
- 2 cups thawed frozen corn kernels
- 1 8 oz. can black beans
- 4 oz. cream cheese
- 1 ½ cup milk
- 1 cup crushed tortilla chips

Directions:

1. Heat the olive oil in a large pan.

2. Sauté the onion and garlic for 5 minutes.

3. Stir the flour, spices, salt and pepper into the pan.

4. Add the broth, picante, cubed potato, corn kernels and beans.

5. Cook for 10 minutes or until the potatoes are cooked and remove from stove.

6. Use a hand mixer to cream the cream cheese and milk.

7. Stir the cream cheese into the corn chowder.

8. Top the chowder with the crush tortilla chips before servings.

Texas-Style Gumbo

Yes, this contains bacon grease. You can use butter but try the bacon grease as an occasional treat. It really makes the dish.

Cooking Time: 2 hours 15 minutes

Servings: 18

Ingredients:

- 1/3 cup bacon grease (eat the bacon for breakfast; you only want the grease)

- 1 cup flour
- ¼ cup chopped scallion
- 4 minced garlic cloves
- ¼ cup sliced okra
- 1 chopped bell pepper
- 3 cups chicken broth
- Salt and pepper to taste
- 1 tbsp. Creole seasoning
- 1 tsp. cayenne pepper
- 2 bay leaves
- 2 cups diced canned tomatoes
- 1 cup chopped crab meat
- 4 lbs. peeled and deveined shrimp
- 1 lb. sliced andouille sausage

Directions:

1. In a large soup pot, heat the bacon fat.

2. Stir in the flour until smooth.

3. Add the scallion, garlic, okra and bell pepper and sauté for 5 minutes.

4. Pour in the broth, tomatoes and all of the seasoning. Stir well.

5. Bring to a boil, then simmer for 2 hours.

6. Add the sliced sausage, crab meat and shrimp and simmer for 10 minutes, or until the shrimp are done.

7. Remove the bay leaves.

8. Serve over rice.

Seafood

Fried Catfish

A different and delicious way to enjoy your fish.

Cooking Time: 10 minutes

Servings: 4

Ingredients:

- 4 catfish fillets
- ¼ cup lime juice
- ¼ cup flour
- ¼ tsp. salt
- ¼ tsp. garlic powder

- ¼ tsp. chili powder
- ¼ tsp. cumin
- Salt and pepper to taste
- 1 cup buttermilk
- 1 cup crushed tortilla chips
- ¼ cup vegetable oil
- 1 cup salsa

Directions:

1. Place the lime juice in a dish.

2. Combine the flour, salt, chili powder, cumin, and garlic powder in another dish.

3. Pour the buttermilk in a third dish and the crushed tortilla chips in a fourth.

4. Dredge the catfish fillets through the lime juice, seasoned flour, buttermilk, and the tortilla chips.

5. Heat the oil in a large skillet.

6. Fry the catfish 5 minutes per side or until flaky.

7. Transfer the fish to a platter and spoon the salsa over each fillet.

Spicy Shrimp Po' Boy

Po'Boys are a southern staple, and this one is nice and spicy.

Cooking Time: 10

Servings: 6

Ingredients:

- 6 French rolls
- 5 tbsp. butter
- 3 beaten eggs
- 2 tbsp Old Bay seasoning

- 1 tsp. creole seasoning
- 1 cup white flour
- 1 ½ cup Panko breadcrumbs
- 2 ½ lbs. peeled and deveined shrimp
- 2 cups canola oil
- ½ shredded head of lettuce

Remoulade sauce:

- ½ cup mayonnaise
- 2 tbsp. mustard
- 1 tbsp. horseradish
- 1 tsp. pickle relish
- 1 teaspoon garlic paste
- Dash of hot sauce
- ¼ cup chopped scallions
- 2 tbsp. soy sauce
- 2 tbsp. lemon juice

Directions:

1. Cut the rolls open and spread them with butter

2. Toast the rolls at 350 degrees for 8 minutes in the oven. Remove.

3. Combine the flour, Old Bay seasoning and creole seasoning in a shallow bowl.

4. Place the breadcrumbs in another bowl.

5. Place the beaten eggs in a third bowl.

6. Dredge the shrimp through the flour, then eggs, and thirdly, the breadcrumbs.

7. Fry the shrimp for 5 minutes each side or until done (depending on side of shrimp).

8. Drain on a paper towel.

9. Combine all the remoulade sauce **Ingredients:**

10. Spread the sauce on the rolls and top with fried shrimp and shredded lettuce.

Veracruz Shrimp

The habanero pepper to HOT. Consider using a whole jalapeno, instead, if you want less heat.

Cooking Time: 25 minutes

Servings: 4

Ingredients:

- 3 tbsp. butter
- 1 diced onion

- 4 minced garlic cloves
- 1 tbsp. capers with a bit of juice
- ¼ cup sliced kalamata olives
- 1 chopped tomato
- ¼ chopped habanero pepper
- ¼ tsp. oregano
- Salt and pepper to taste
- 3 tbsp. fish broth
- 3 tbsp. white wine
- 20 large shrimp
- 1 cup cilantro

Directions:

Heat the butter in a skillet.

Sauté the onion for 5 minutes.

Add the garlic and capers, olives, chopped pepper, diced tomatoes, broth and wine.

Simmer for 10 minutes.

Season with oregano, salt and pepper.

Add the shrimp to the skillet and cook for 10 minutes, until the shrimp is done.

Top with cilantro

Sides

Coleslaw

Perfect for a Texas-style BBQ. Pro Tip: When wrapped in a tortilla, this makes a great veggie wrap. Or add some shredded cooked chicken for a chicken wrap.

Cooking Time: 0

Servings: 8

Ingredients:

- 1 cup mayonnaise
- 1 tbsp. lime juice

- 1 tsp. cumin
- 1 tsp. cayenne pepper
- Salt and pepper to taste
- 1 bag of coleslaw mix
- 1 seeded and minced jalapeno pepper
- 3 tbsp. chopped onion
- 2 tbsp. sugar

Directions:

1. Whisk together the mayonnaise, lime juice, cumin, cayenne pepper, salt and pepper.

2. Combine the coleslaw mix, jalapeno pepper, onion and sugar.

3. Toss the coleslaw with the dressing.

4. Refrigerate for 1 hour.

Tex-Mex Corn

This corn side dish both rich and spicy. Perfect for a Mexican-themed dinner.

Cooking Time: 45 minutes

Servings: 8

Ingredients:

- 8 oz. cream cheese
- 1/3 cup butter
- ½ cup heavy cream
- 2 cups frozen corn
- 2 minced garlic cloves

- 1 diced red bell pepper
- 4 oz. canned chopped green chilis
- 2 tsp. creole seasoning or to taste
- ½ tsp. cumin
- Salt and pepper to taste

Directions:

1. Preheat the oven to 350 degrees.

2. Heat the cream cheese and butter in a pan until they melt.

3. Stir in the milk for a smooth sauce.

4. Place the corn, minced garlic, bell pepper, chopped chili peppers in a baking dish and combine.

5. Add the creole seasoning, cumin, salt and pepper and stir.

6. Top with the sauce.

7. Bake for 40 minutes

Jalapeno Yams

If you're tired of overly sweet yams, this recipe is for you.

Cooking Time: 1 hour 20 minutes

Servings: 4

Ingredients:

- 2 large yams
- 1 jalapeno pepper
- 1 tbsp. chopped shallots
- 3 tbsp. butter
- 3 tbsp. orange juice
- Salt and pepper to taste
- ¼ cup chopped pecans

Directions:

1. Preheat the oven to 350 degrees.

2. Bake the yams for 1 hour, depending on size.

3. 20 minutes before the yams are done, place the jalapeno in the oven.

4. Peel and mash both the yam and jalapeno pepper in a bowl.

5. Stir in the butter and orange juice.

6. Use a hand mixer to create a smooth consistency.

7. Season with salt and pepper.

8. Place the yams in a baking dish and top with the chopped pecans.

9. Bake for 20 minutes.

Ranch Potato Salad

This potato salad is fantastic at any bar-b-que.

Cooking Time: 15 minutes

Servings: 16

Ingredients:

- 5 lb. small potatoes
- 1 lb. bacon
- ½ oz. packaged ranch dressing mix

- 1 cup mayonnaise
- 1 cup sour cream
- Salt and pepper to taste
- ½ tsp chili powder

Directions:

1. Cook the potatoes in a pot of salted water for 15 minutes.

2. Let the potatoes cool, then peel and cube them.

3. While the potatoes cook, fry the bacon in a skillet to desired crispness, about 10 minutes.

4. Drain the bacon on a paper towel and crumble.

5. Combine the mayonnaise, sour cream, and ranch dressing in a bowl.

6. Toss the potatoes with the dressing.

7. Season the potato salad with salt, pepper and chili powder.

8. Top with the crumbled bacon and refrigerate for at least 1 hour.

Pinto Beans

This is the Texas version of Boston Beans.

Cooking Time: 2 hours

Servings: 8

Ingredients:

- 1lb. dry pinto beans
- 3 ½ cup chicken broth
- 1 chopped onion
- 1 chopped jalapeno pepper

- 3 minced garlic cloves
- 1/3 cup red salsa
- 4 oz. chopped chipotle peppers in adobo sauce
- 1 tsp. cumin
- Salt and pepper to taste

Directions:

1. Soak the pinto beans in water overnight.

2. Place all ingredients in a pot.

3. Bring the broth to a boil, then reduce the heat to low.

4. Cook for 2 hours.

5. Keep an eye on the liquid and add more if needed.

Dessert

Oatmeal Cookies

Sometimes, even a tough cowboy or cowgirl just wants a cookie. This oatmeal cookie is tasty without being too sweet.

Cooking Time: 12 minutes

Servings: 20

- 2 ½ cups white flour
- ½ tsp. baking powder

- 1 tsp. baking soda
- ½ tsp. salt
- 1 tsp. cinnamon
- ½ cup butter
- ½ cup canola oil or coconut oil
- 2 cups brown sugar
- 2 tbsp. honey
- 1 tsp. vanilla extract
- 2 eggs
- 3 cups quick cooking oats
- 1 cup chopped walnuts

Directions:

1. Preheat the oven to 350 degrees.

2. Combine the flour, baking powder, baking soda and cinnamon and set aside.

3. Use a hand mixer to whip the butter, oil, sugar, vanilla extract and honey until smooth.

4. Add the eggs one at a time.

5. Slowly add the flour to the butter ingredients.

6. Stir well and add the oats and chopped walnuts.

7. Drop tsp-sized batter on a baking sheet.

8. Bake for 12 minutes.

Texas Sheet Cake

Sheet cakes are large, which is probably why they are so popular in the large state of Texas. It serves an entire crew or a whole BBQ gang.

Cooking Time: 20 minutes

Servings: 18

Ingredients:

- 2 cups white flour
- 2 cups white sugar

- 1 tsp. baking soda
- Salt to taste
- ¾ cup sour cream
- 2 eggs
- ½ tsp. almond extract
- 1 cup butter
- 1 cup strong black coffee
- 1 cup unsweetened cocoa powder

Frosting

- ¾ cup milk
- ¾ cup unsweetened cocoa powder
- ½ cup butter
- 4 cups confectioners' sugar
- ½ tsp. almond extract

Directions:

1. Preheat the oven to 350 degrees.

2. Lightly butter a 9 x 13 cake pan.

3. Stir together the flour, sugar, baking soda and salt.

4. Beat the sour cream, eggs and almond extract. Set aside.

5. Heat the butter in a small pan and stir in the coffee and cocoa. Stir until creamy.

6. Let the cocoa/butter cool, then slowly add to the eggs.

7. Transfer the batter to the baking dish.

8. Bake for 20 minutes.

Printed in Great Britain
by Amazon